STRESS TO STRENGTH

Mind Tools to Calm, Connect and Create

DR JUDY HINWOOD

EAM Publishing

STRESS TO STRENGTH
Mind Tools to Calm, Connect and Create

Dr Judy Hinwood

Website: www.StresstoStrength.com

Published by

EAM Publishing

PO Box 4125

Forest Lake, Qld, 4078 Australia

Phone: +61 7 3879 0069

Email: admin@StresstoStrength.com

Copyright © 2013 by Dr Judy Hinwood

All rights reserved. No part of this book may be reproduced or transmitted in any form or by any means, electronic or mechanical, including photocopying, recording, or by any information storage and retrieval system without the written permission of the publisher, except where permitted by law.

ISBN: 978-0-9872805-6-5

Cover design by: idrewdesign

Why not use Drs John & Judy Hinwood as guest speakers for your next conference or seminar?

STRESS TO STRENGTH

PO Box 4125, Forest Lake 4078, Queensland, AUSTRALIA
Tel: +61 7 3879 0069
Fax: +61 7 3714 9700
Email: info@StresstoStrength.com
Website: www.StresstoStrength.com

Drs John & Judy Hinwood have an unusual way of changing people's lives. In a journey over the past 26 years they have been handing out a small white card to people they have met. The card has just three words written on it ... **"Expect A Miracle"**. They have handed out over 95,000 cards to people all over the world in the last 26 years. Through this small act of giving the Hinwood's prompt people to think about their own miracles; the small, seemingly insignificant events and moments in people's lives that open the doors to a sense of wonderment and opportunity.

John & Judy Hinwood are sought-after international conference speakers and they run public events all over the world.

As international speakers they inspire their audiences into taking practical action steps to move their lives to new levels. Their perspectives, humour, observations, insights into life and entertaining stories are from the heart and they inspire and motivate people into taking positive action steps.

The inspirational You Can EXPECT A MIRACLE book series are giving many people around the world hope and a good dose of positivity.

Also by Drs John & Judy Hinwood

Expect A Miracle Cards

Expect A Miracle card packs

Live Events

Creating Miracles In Your Life (1 hour)

The Miracle Mindset (2 hours)

Expect A Miracle School (Half Day)

Stress to Strength Workshop (3 Days)

Webinars ... Streamed

Creating Miracles in Your Life

The Miracle Mindset

Expect A Miracle School

Books

You Can EXPECT A MIRACLE ... The Book To Change Your Life

You Can EXPECT A MIRACLE ... Yes YOU Can

You Can EXPECT A MIRACLE ... Unexpected Miracles

You Can EXPECT A MIRACLE ... With Chiropractic

You Can EXPECT A MIRACLE ... Insights Into Life

You Can EXPECT A MIRACLE ... 201 Miracle Messages from A to Z

You Can EXPECT AMIRACLE ...13 Keys to Becoming A Miracle Magnet

Audio Programs ... CD & Streamed

Creating Miracles in Your Life

The Miracle Mindset

Expect A Miracle School

Online Programs

Stress to Strength Alliance ... Via email and webinar

Stress to Strength ... Powerful Steps – 23 days

Stress to Strength ... Final Keys – 49 days

Stress to Strength Coaching Program

Practitioner Training

Stress to Strength Practitioner ... 12 month Cert IV program

www.StresstoStrength.com

I dedicate this book with great gratitude to:

All people seeking to transform their lives from Stress to Strength and who are willing to take action to achieve this outcome.

All people seeking closer connection and communion with the Creator.

All people open to exploring the wonders in our minds and in our potentials.

Acknowledgements

My gratitude knows no bounds for the continual availability of Gerard, my spiritual guide. I have been blessed for about thirty years to have had unlimited access to his wisdom, love and generosity of spirit. Whatever my challenges, I have been given tools to manage, learn, move on, and thrive.

My wonderful friend, the late Yvonne Davies of Brisbane, has been absolutely instrumental in making sure I have the tools clearly defined, and I am thankful past any words for her love, laughter, commitment, unhesitating friendship and availability. Her daughter, Linn Davies ably succeeds her.

I am honored and blessed to be married to the brilliant, endlessly giving and caring Dr John Hinwood, chiropractor, mentor, author and speaker, and to be part of our loving, encompassing family. My dear parents Doris and Wilf Armitage of Bega were great, generous and kind teachers to the last. To all of you and to our caring, supportive and faithful friends, my boundless thanks.

Thank you to Dianne Girot, Christine Alexson and John Milne who have edited and made suggestions during the preparation of the manuscript and to my friends Patricia Rose and Isobel Johnstone who also provided editing support and encouragement. Dr Joe Dispensa has given invaluable advice also.

Also a big thank you to Deborah Lloyd, multimedia designer and artist for her cleverness, especially when the technical stuff was all too hard for my right brain focused mind.

Special thanks to Drew of Iidrewdesigns for the peace and serenity his cover design creates for the reader.

To the many, many teachers who have invested their precious time and life energy in me, my deep gratitude to each of you.

Introduction

We are powerful beyond measure. We are totally capable of designing and creating the life that fulfils our desires and our potentials. We come from energy, we are energy and we have a birthright to access and use that creative energy at will, for whatever we wish. We impose boundaries on ourselves by not using our thoughts and imaginations to reach forward. It is true for me that thoughts are real forces, so my power to think creatively and positively is my power to create my life.

In my experience the mind makes our life heaven or hell because we choose in each moment how we think and feel and our attitude, creating energy that will help us or hinder us, making us happy or sad in the process. So, we create our own state of being, our own life and health in every moment.

In our humanness our fears and doubts are where our harnesses and lessons are. The extent we control and re-create these into forward moving energies, is the extent we control our lives. How sad that people believe they have to, or are even destined to, stay in bad and sad circumstances, while living in wonderful countries like Australia. I have been there and it's not necessary to stay there.

We have the power in each moment to shape our lives, you and I, into the brilliance we wish – thought by thought, picture by picture, action by action. As I see it, realizing our dreams and goals is simply a function of the number of action steps we are willing and able to take in an amount of time. We all can make something better of our health and lives.

There is nothing more powerful than the energy of creation, the Source, Life Force, Love, Innate Intelligence, Higher Authority, Nature, Spirit, the Creator, the Great I Am, Essence, God. Whatever your name or concept for the power that created all, I encourage you to simply insert that instead of the name I will use, 'the White Light' or 'the Light'. This is the power available to us, whatever the name you use.

The 'White Light' or 'the Light' is the concept that suits me but is by no means prescriptive. Each of you, no matter what religion or spiritual beliefs you hold, can simply insert your own pictures, feelings and concepts into the tools and accompanying information to make them relevant for you. I smile to think 'God' would be delighted if those of us from varying beliefs could unite in such a simple way so we can move forward in greater harmony, unity and love. Because, what else is there, really, after all our humanness is stripped away?

How interesting is the knowledge that thoughts and feelings affect our body. Fear, guilt, resentment, sadness and doubts, for example, are energies that negatively reflect in the cells of our bodies and produce dis-harmony, and even dis-ease. Thoughts are real forces and the mind is in every cell of our bodies. I am so grateful for the wealth of information from scientists who are making such inroads into how this actually happens.

Signs and symptoms in our bodies are signposts pointing to where we are off track in our thinking, feelings and behaviours. They are very helpful signposts so we can do something about our health and life, which are intertwined, as they actually point to where to go to add more life energy. I'm so grateful for what I learnt about this from having cancer long ago and having my body healed naturally.

Stress is normal and natural for us to move ahead with our lives and there is a part of the Autonomic nervous System that activates our body for the stress. However, the other side of that Autonomic Nervous System is the part that slows us down and restores the body to calm, cleans it and relaxes it. When we are stressed for too long or too often chemical changes happen in the body that aren't healthy – and we are on our way to problems. It is absolutely essential to us in so many ways that we give ourselves the gift of quiet, relaxation, self-healing and stress management, as with the use of the tools in this guidebook. I've put more information for you on my website www.StresstoStrength.com.

But what I believe is only important to me! It is completely irrelevant to you and your life - unless the information in this book rings true for you. If you find truths here, then fine, if not, then fine. Your truths must be your truths, felt in your heart, soul, intuition, and your mind. If we share some truths, please make the tools your own and relevant to your life.

You may think the tools sound too simple to work? In this day and age we sometimes seem to need complexity or we judge the data not valid. That doesn't work for me. I really can't see complexity as necessary because these tools do work. Especially when used with 'that P word', patience. Simplicity also works!

I have been invaluably assisted in my life by these tools and words. Many challenges have been eased and simplified by using the suggestions in this handbook from child raising, to business and health, to relationships. I see the tools as sustainable self care strategies and as true gifts.

These tools have been invaluable to me to recreate a healthy body for myself a few times, to create my life dreams many times, and many clients have loved them also. I value the calm and peace produced by these gifts beyond words. Please be kind to yourself as you learn to use them as each of you will have your own perfect pace.

As you move through the book you will find a tool or strategy described, then followed by words of encouragement, illumination and discussion that have applied to that tool for me, labeled Conversation.

Not all the tools will suit you. We are made blessedly unique with gifts differing. What will suit an analytical mind may not suit a more kinesthetic person; a more social person may not suit the same tools as an introverted person. I recommend that to benefit from these tools you stay open, and don't judge yourself and others, so you can find *your* way to what suits you.

There is no right/wrong about the tools' use. Your uniqueness will determine what will be best for you in any moment and the results gained. As a general rule, The White Light tool can be used at any time of day or night as often as we think of it, eyes open or closed as it gives us great calm and energy. The White Light should be used before any closed eye process, meditation and tool.

The others, use singly or in any combination you wish. For example, I like The White Light, then The Face or The Purple Crystal before any quiet time or meditation.

Healing Visualizations are used to create images in your mind of the health you really want. They can be done daily for a few minutes for body and mind cleaning, or more in times of illness – as much as you feel you need, really. The

Mind Tools to Calm, Connect and Create

visualizations are really 'inductions' or 'imageries' as they install images in the mind that create change, but for clarity I've called them 'visualizations'

I use The Face quickly on its own as a memory jogger for an answer to come to me, and when I've used the White Light tool in combination with The Face, I find it is really helpful for focus on a task.

Consistency is really basic for progress in the mind and spiritual realms. Practice and repetition bring surprising and delightful rewards. Just 5 minutes of quiet each day will do in the beginning if you want to bring in more peace, calm, balance and harmony. The more you read and use the tools, the more you will absorb and fill your body and spirit with life force, and re-create yourself and your life.

Some tools and discussion in this handbook are similar, and that is because we are so human that we may need to hear information a bit differently, or have it repeated, for it to penetrate through any layers of resistance to change.

Your individual results with this work are your own wonderful adventure and your responsibility to make happen. While these tools and strategies have been, and are, effective for myself and many others I can take no responsibility for your use of them or your outcomes from them. I would love to guarantee their effectiveness for you, but sadly I am not in your living room with you to lead you personally if you hit slow times and give up. These tools and conversations are not medical treatments. More help is available on my website, www.StresstoStrength.com, though I do believe you can achieve excellent results on your own.

It is in a spirit of love and gratitude that I share this

profound information, with trust that your innate wisdom will lead you to the pages you need to open in the moment, whether for peace, encouragement, better health, higher energy, more love, understanding, strength or simply for learning.

I commend the words to you. May they bring hope in any dark hours, lead you out into healthier places, invigorate the good times and give you more peace, meaning and freedom in your life.

Dr Judy Hinwood

Table of Contents

Acknowledgements 8
Introduction 11

PART 1: Peace Tools 21
The Universal Tool 22
The Universal Tool Conversation 24
The Face 26
The Face Conversation 27
Lotus Blossom 28
The Lotus Blossom Conversation 29
The Giant Pyramid 30
The Giant Pyramid Conversation 31
The Blazer 33
The Blazer Conversation 34
The Mirror 36
Mirror Conversation 37
The White Rose 39
The White Rose Conversation 40
The Purple Crystal 41
The Purple Crystal Conversation 42
A Pair of Earphones 44
A Pair of Earphones Conversation 45
The Fountain 46
The Fountain Conversation 47
The Internal Alarm Clock 49
The Internal Alarm Clock Conversation 50
The Ball of Clarity 52

The Ball of Clarity Conversation 54

PART 2: Life Tools **55**
The Chrysanthemum..56
The Chrysanthemum Conversation..57
A 'Clean Slate' 59
A 'Clean Slate' Conversation..60
The White Rope..62
The White Rope Conversation 63
The Tall Grass...65
The Tall Grass Conversation 66
The Torch 67
The Torch Conversation..68
The Abundance Bowl 70
The Abundance Bowl Conversation 71
The Whistle...73
The Whistle Conversation 74
The Worry Beads..76
The Worry Beads Conversation 77
A Gift of Joy 79
A Gift of Joy Conversation 80
The Chariot 82
The Chariot Conversation 83
The Gold Medal 85
The Gold Medal Conversation...87
What a Bunch of Flowers!..89
What a Bunch of Flowers! Conversation...................................90
The Ball of Arcs 92

The Ball of Arcs Conversation 93
The Crown 95
The Crown Conversation 96
The Life Jacket 98
The Life Jacket Conversation 99

PART 3: Health Tools 101
Healing Visualizations 102
Healing Visualizations Conversation 104
In My Palm 106
In My Palm Conversation 107
The White Flame 109
The White Flame Conversation 110
The Motivation Pills 111
The Motivation Pills Conversation 112
Dancing Free 114
Dancing Free Conversation 116
The Flotation Tank 117
The Flotation Tank Conversation 118
The Angels' Wings 120
The Angels' Wings Conversation 121
The Box of Stardust 122
The Box of Stardust Conversation 123
About the Author 125

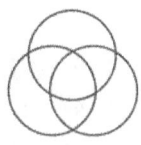

PART 1: Peace Tools

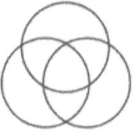

The Universal Tool

Sit quietly in a comfortable chair, feet and arms uncrossed.

Relax into your chair. Use the affirmation on the adjacent page to invoke the Light.

Above your head is a brilliant White Light. Imagine it any way you wish; see it, feel it, know it or just think of it. You may imagine it as a gentle snowfall, a white shower, a set of stadium lights, light shimmering off a sunny lake, a brilliant snow field, or any way you wish.

Allow The Light to flow quietly and easily down and around you, surrounding you like an eggshell of protection and love.

Allow the Light to flow slowly down through your head and down through your body filling you with calm, safety, peace and love.

Focus gently on your body's centre, your energy centre at your solar plexus. There is a well of energy there that we can deplete over time or in stressful situations. Simply shine a bright Light in there and fill your energy up to overflowing again, allowing the Light to radiate out to fill your body.

Sit in this eternal, gentle, soothing space. Know you are being healed and cleansed by the Source, physically, mentally, emotionally and spiritually.

This process 'takes as long as it takes' to reach the point of calm or peace.

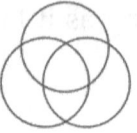

The Universal Tool Conversation

Think of the white Light as pure energy in a most positive form There is nothing more powerful than 'what is', the essence of us, the creative force, the ongoing spirit.

The tool to invoke the Light is this affirmation. 'I bless and receive the. Great White Light of Divine protection and love and give thanks that it now surrounds me and encompasses me and flows forth with me'.

This could be your main affirmation, your mantra. Say it with fervor and depth. Really mean it. It is very important to invoke The Light before any meditation. Say it also before going into a difficult situation or whenever you feel the necessity. Invoke the Light before you set a foot out of bed, and before you go to sleep, before going into danger like in your car. Invoke the Light before using any of the tools in this handbook, please.

This tool uses the power of Source, of Life, of Creation. We all come from that life energy and have it flowing through us, and we are at liberty to access it for our own good. It is part of our birthright to use the Light to enhance our lives as we choose – we are in it, we are of it, we are connected to it, we are all networked, it is ours to use creatively.

Remember, too, that the White Light is something you can use to diffuse other peoples' angers and animosities. Surround them with the Light. It is a very special gift. Use it and you will find it will be of great benefit to you, and the more you use it, the more it will grow within you.

The Light can be a blessing of love and light you spread around you to cocoon you so you can feel protected and safe and secure, knowing that the outside negativity of the world around you does not have to enter you and affect your energy.

Look forward with awareness. Walk purposefully into the Light and you will find peace and calm. Lock it into your heart so you may bring it out in times of stress, and know it is always there. It is your balm, your salve to help you always.

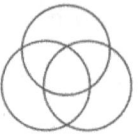

The Face

Sit quietly, feel your body contacting the chair, allow surrounding sounds to just be. White Light yourself.

Take one hand in front of your face, just below the level of your chin, palm down. Notice your thoughts – they are probably occupying most of your head.

Gently lift that hand up past your chin, slowly up and up, while the thoughts stay above the hand as it moves. Below the hand, space, peace and calm are revealed. Take your time lifting the hand to the top of your face with the thoughts still above it.

Allow your thoughts to do what they do; they are not your focus. Your thoughts have another place to be, and as you look forward, you have soul space in which to be blessedly still. In a while you will notice quiet and calm in your whole body.

If you wish you may let the thoughts go, perhaps by lifting a lid, and they can float out and away. It is irrelevant what they do.

Leaving the hand at the top of the forehead is easier when we start this technique. Later, imagining the hand is enough.

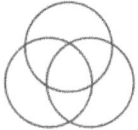

The Face Conversation

This tool, 'the Face' always gives me peace and centers me, whether I'm in the middle of busyness or other challenges. A main key is this: give yourself the gift of quietly sitting for five minutes at least each day to regenerate and focus on calm, on your Self. With practice just the thought of 'The Face' will give the same effect rapidly, with your eyes open, while you are living your life.

In meditation, when you don't seek, the answers will come. Ask for communication, but don't seek it, rather, use the time as relaxation. Allow the free flow of information. It will be a time of body boost and repair, while the mind can free itself of the chatter. The cobwebs cluttering the intuitive channels will fly away.

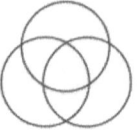

Lotus Blossom

When needing peace, close your eyes and visualize very deeply and with great feeling, the beauty of a lotus blossom.

See it at your feet and see yourself at the centre of the lotus, coming in to your full bloom at the very centre of this lotus blossom of peace.

As the flower unfolds and comes into its' full bloom you will see that the centre of the lotus is in truth a brilliant white light which comes up and encases you in its' peace and its' light.

Feel the warmth of this light, smell the perfume of the blossom, feel the velvet touch of the petals under your feet and take those sensations with you. Wind those feelings around you with the light.

Take these and exalt in them. Breathe in the light and the softness and feel them go throughout your entire being. Feel them being taken into your body and radiating from it.

As well as encasing the outer body they are flowing through the inner body, filling you with warmth and peace and love.

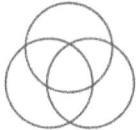

The Lotus Blossom Conversation

The gift today is pure love. Feel a gentle hand on your head and understand that this is a hand of love, understanding and light.

You are given this as a gift to lighten your burden, to bring you peace, to bring you comfort in times of worry, of indecision, of problems, or just day to day living.

Think once more of the hand upon your head and feel the glow of the light that flows from it to you. Allow its' peace to permeate your mind and heart, and ultimately your whole being.

As this love and light flows through you, allow it also to radiate out from you, and embrace those close to you.

When you need a helping hand over life's potholes that are necessary along the pathway, reach for the caring hand. If you stumble and fall, understand that this hand of friendship and love is there ready to take your hand at any time. It is always there, just within your reach.

Rejoice in the potholes, in the lessons. At times they could appear meaningless or too hard to handle. But everything has a purpose and ultimate result even though they may not be apparent.

Take these gifts with love and a very earnest desire of peace for you.

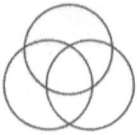

The Giant Pyramid

See a giant Pyramid above your home, a shimmering white force field and as people step over the threshold an instant calm comes over them and the whole home.

See everything under the pyramid living in peace and harmony.

The pyramid also fosters the energies of good ideas and pushes you forward.

It gives you the energy needed to sustain the pace you need to fulfil your goals and dreams.

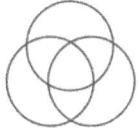

The Giant Pyramid Conversation

The ambition to have peaceful relationships is a wonderful aim, a wonderful ambition, a wonderful way of thinking. But many changes may have to happen within yourself to bring this about.

In dealing with relationships you must understand the other persons' point of view may not coincide with yours. There will be many times when working with such an ambition that you will have to let things slide, so to speak. You will have to let things that would normally cause you to react, fail to cause a reaction. Understand that these are the differences that make one person them, and you, you.

There are ideas and principles you will need to focus on in working towards more harmonious and peaceful relationships; understanding and respecting the other persons' differences, understanding and respecting their will to do as they wish, not to do as you would have them do. Understanding and respecting the very, very great differences between people and not allowing these to interfere with the relationship or the friendship, or whatever; but rather, accepting and seeing that these differences are alright for them, so they are alright for you. Their choices may not be your choices. Seeing that you cannot influence them or change their mind without taking away their free will is essential.

They, of course, will then treat you the same way. No two

people are created the same; no two people have identical personalities, identical dreams, or aspirations, desires, mentality or abilities. All are perfectly created differently and they are like pieces in a jigsaw puzzle fitting in to one another, for one's weakness will be another's strength and ones' strength another's weakness. This is necessary to bring about balance and understanding, peace and harmony in relationships. Accepting each person and not trying to make them carbon copies of yourself, but rather, allowing them to be their own individual fish in the pond, their own piece of the jigsaw puzzle, is needed.

When you understand this and work on the principle, you will indeed be working towards the peace and harmony that you seek. When you fail to react, but rather accept, you will find peace and harmony will become your second nature.

You will find this will work in every relationship, whether it is your spouse, your children, your workplace or people you meet along the way.

Part 1 : Peace Tools

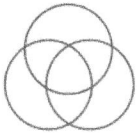

The Blazer

When wondering if guidance is near, imagine a pure white blazer with blue bands around the sleeves and blue buttons, and pull it on. When you want to be sure information is from the highest source, put the blazer on, feel the warmth of it, see it in its brilliance.

When you feel negative, confused or out of sorts, take the blazer, put it on and feel courage, strength and positivity, or whatever you need at the time, coming to you.

When you need to be reminded of these words and have an understanding of them, put on the blazer and in doing so you will completely enfold yourself in love and purest White Light.

Be sure of the strength of both this gift and the Light and feel the strength of both throughout your days. Allow this to bring love and peace into your heart and extend that to those around you.

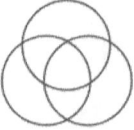

The Blazer Conversation

We all think at times we are isolated little units and everything revolves around us and our little world.

Instead, see the connections between us like an octopus whose tentacles spread out so everything acts and interacts upon the other forming this incredible network that is life.

If you can imagine all these different strings going in all different directions with you here as a central figure in your life, linking up to all the other central figures, this is what life is all about.

Things really do not happen often by chance or accident, even things that look like they are disastrous, and you think 'why did Life let me do this or that?' or 'why did this happen to me?' Ultimately, you will see how somehow or other it has happened to affect you or affect another specifically. You may not see why in your particular life that you have to go through something, but if you could see at the other end of the tentacle, you would see how what has happened here with you has changed that persons' life over there. So you see, when one thing acts on another, it brings about a chain reaction

Never doubt or become dissatisfied or upset if you think you have been given the short end of the rope because it may be short on one hand, but the next time, you will get the long end. It's all part and parcel of this crazy and incredible web of life, of one person affecting another.

When you can understand this it will make things more bearable for you when you have been the one chosen to help another in this way. Generally Life tries to even things out, and you try to even it out when you choose your life, but occasionally it just does not even out.

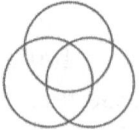

The Mirror

Each morning look closely at yourself in a mirror.

Look for 2-7 minutes. Look deeply into your eyes. Do it for two weeks at least, every day. If you start to feel irritation, push through it. Keep going to release the energies that are probably from low self esteem. Start at 30 seconds if you have to.

Affirm 'I love myself unconditionally, I forgive myself, I respect myself'

Affirm 'I am a wonderful being of White Light, perfectly Pure and beautiful'

Repeat one or both of these at least a few times within the time you give yourself.

Or simply say 'I love you' to yourself, looking into your eyes.

See yourself as the good spirit that you are. See all that you are. See the great qualities you have. See all you have accomplished in your life – and no, they do not have to be big things.

This tool will remind you of the wonderful person you are. This is not ego; it is to promote self worth, without which we limit our lives.

Keep on with the exercise until you really believe the words. This can take some time as so many of us carry resistance to these positive thoughts of ourselves.

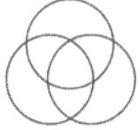

Mirror Conversation

This mirror concept is worth examining. That which we see in others is actually a reflection of ourselves. For example, if we see someone as critical, we are being critical,

Many people think the reflection has to be an exact sameness, but that is not always so. Maybe it is just saying beware, this could be you if you are not careful, maybe it is just a distorted view.

You must look at this in different ways. For example, if you see someone being aggressive, check if you own that aggression, if you are being aggressive. Watch the encounter and learn so that next time you come across such a situation, you will have learnt not to handle it in an aggressive manner. That is a side of you that you choose not to use.

Look and see what the mirror is trying to tell you. Maybe it is a situation where you need to show a little understanding or a little kindness, perhaps to yourself.

This Mirror tool has been a most difficult technique for me but it really works when I use it.

I had many attempts to do this each morning, but each time I just didn't continue. This is classically from feeling badly about ourselves, and I urge you to persevere; just make time to do this, through tears, through self doubt, through a prolonged 'Oh, sure…' as you just know 'the affirmations are rubbish – after all, how can I forgive myself for…'

Use it till you have no energy around the words for some days and you are harmonious with them. If it doesn't work for you, don't be concerned, use any of the other tools you want to as they all ease our way and clear up any layers of mental and emotional baggage we may have accumulated. Later you may be inspired to have another go at 'The Mirror".

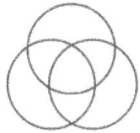

The White Rose

This gift is a beautiful white rose.

See the rose as the emblem of love, peace and tranquility that is extended to you.

Imagine smelling the rose, savoring the perfume. Look at the rose and see its beauty and perfection. See this as being you and how your Creator views you.

See the petals of the rose and see them as being the outside casing of you, just as your body is the outside casing of your spirit.

Understand that the beauty and the fragrance of the rose is contained within, so irrespective of the outside appearance, the beauty, the perfume and true essence of love is the core of you.

Recognize your inner beauty that is surely there, and your spiritual perfection. Recognize it, rejoice in it and understand it. That is why you are given this rose today.

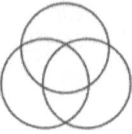

The White Rose Conversation

When wondering which thoughts are from your intuition, watch for the very first thought that comes unsolicited into your mind, the very first thought.

Then, close your eyes and establish the White Light. It may not be a complete visionary White Light to start with; you may only be able to manage a white dot or flash like lightning, but it will be there if you look for it.

Keep practicing and the Light will expand. Our gift for doing this varies so much from person to person, it is really important not to be discouraged if it takes a while.

If that flash of light comes with body heat that will give double confirmation you are accessing your intuition.

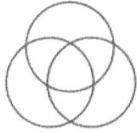

The Purple Crystal

What a beautiful gift, a beautiful purple crystal. Whenever you sit in your meditation chair imagine this gem, the size of an apricot, and put it between your eyes, just on your forehead. This energy area is known as the 3rd eye. Allow the crystal to 'attach' there for the meditation and it will assist with your focus to make the meditation deeper and easier.

See it in your mind's eye and do it every time. You will find that your focus is clearer and sharper and you will be able to remember what you have meditated about and what you have received in meditation.

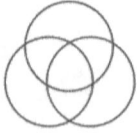

The Purple Crystal Conversation

It is your responsibility to be as happy as possible. This is taking responsibility for yourself.

Accepting whatever you have done, whether it be 'right' or the 'wrong' is taking responsibility for yourself.

Accepting the fact that you are not perfect, accepting that you will make mistakes, is taking responsibility for yourself.

Not blaming your actions on other people or circumstances or events is taking responsibility for yourself.

And being happy while you are doing these three is your responsibility. If you want to be happy, that depends on you, not the children, not your husband, or work situation or anything else – it depends on you inside and how you view things. There are people who do every necessary job on the planet and are quite happy to do it. This happiness is part of their being and they would find happiness in whatever they are doing – or not another dish would be washed! People can and do find enjoyment in doing anything. This is not forced; it is something inside of them.

Be happy and contented with you, first of all, and then you will be happy and contented with the things around you and your work. That is taking responsibility for yourself and your actions.

Yes, there are other responsibilities – to your spouse, your children, your work and these should be a joy also and not a chore. You must look to ways you can make life more joyous for yourself, and then it is more joyous for them also.

If a person is not happy in their work then they should look for other employment. It is not part of any learning process that they should continue in employment that brings dissatisfaction to them. All that does is bring up negativity in them and makes them disgruntled with life as a whole. Why should a third of your life be spent in misery when there are probably other things out there you are more suited to that will give you much more pleasure? Life is not meant to be one of servitude to things that are unpleasant, but rather, one of enjoying the journey of life by doing as many things as possible that bring you pleasure. Huge sacrifices are made by many, for example, a single Mum who simply has to continue in a job she dislikes to care for her children. Perhaps she could set goals for when she can free herself a bit, like setting her sights on a course to increase her skills, and using these tools to stay as centered, powerful, joyful and healthy as she can.

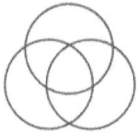

A Pair of Earphones

Before meditation, White Light yourself as always, then see yourself physically picking up a pair of earphones and putting them on, and then starting your meditation.

Know that when you start your meditation with the earphones on you will hear your intuition more clearly.

Also, using these each time you meditate can help focus your mind on quiet and calm by blocking out noise – yes, it is useful.

Use this gift for it is given out of love, with excited anticipation of your wonderful results in quietening your mind and spirit.

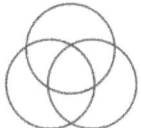

A Pair of Earphones Conversation

Another tool you might choose to use is this one, A Pair of Earphones. This is useful when there are a lot of things happening in my world, if my mind is racing, and if finding my inner quiet is not easy. Then I can ask a question and know or hear the answer and know it is not my mind playing tricks on me, but my intuition.

Try to listen to what your intuition tells you. Your first thought before your conscious mind kicks in is your intuition.

Have full faith in what it tells you and work with what you are given.

However, use also what you have thought out for yourself.

You have your own God given mind to work things out for yourself. Look and recognize what options are open for you, weigh up your options, think clearly and balance that with your intuitive knowledge.

Things that come to you show you that you can rely on your intuition, but they make you use your own mind and your own tools to work out your solutions.

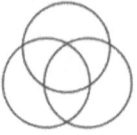

The Fountain

Sit quietly. Imagine a fountain, a fountain spraying out a rosette of water gently from its' centre.

When that fountain sprays out its water, imagine that the water is any tears that need to be shed. This will give you closure on any grief and sadness that surrounds you or that you are carrying.

See this freeing fountain, knowing that things are going to be better with the washing away of previously unshed tears.

As the drops fall from the fountain, feel them run down your cheeks, releasing the grief from within, and feel yourself more calm at last.

You may release physical tears, or you may not. Whichever happens, know the tool is working as the energy of the emotion is released just by your thinking that it is so through the fountain.

Thoughts are real energy so you have created your own release. By all means do this as often as you need to feel better. The exercise below in discussion will help you relax and let go if you need.

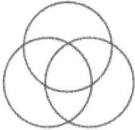

The Fountain Conversation

A mind can wind up, much like an over-wound watch spring. It is so taut that when you start to relax all the stored up thoughts start running through your mind, being thrown up to be handled, making it difficult to concentrate and still the mind. You think of things you could do, and things you are doing and things you did do. It takes a great deal of willpower, effort and discipline to overcome this blockage to become quiet and calm.

Another visualization to release stress:

Start by feeling your body in your chair and noticing your breathing. Then imagine all the excess thoughts going from your head down through your arms and out your resting hands. Visualize all those wayward thoughts draining away and out, perhaps into a white balloon. Allow the mind to go still. Don't try to focus strongly on any one thing as this brings up the action of your mind, but rather, allow the mind to float freely Gently bring the mind back to your breathing if it wanders.

Try to rise, self, soul, essence, floating free of your body, hovering over your body. This will take your mind off the stressful things and take the soul to a place where it can look down at the rest of the people. It can go to a peaceful place where you can lie on the grass and gaze at the sky, watch the movement in the clouds and see them take different shapes and forms. Don't try to think of anything definite at this time, just allow everything to flow and be free. When you tire of that scene among the stars, look around you and enjoy the peace and calm.

Try these methods and do not despair. Try to sit or lie with limbs uncrossed. You will learn to relax and enjoy these postures in time. Once you can relax the mind, all else becomes clear, all else becomes easier. Eventually everyone can do this, truly. Times vary from immediately to soon.

What an odd concept – this is, wasting time. It is not wasting time when you are doing something for your own benefit, and benefiting your own body like resting. This is all within the programming of your own mind. You must work out the blockage; have the will and determination to do this. A good exercise to do this is to affirm in writing, with feeling, "I am peaceful and joyful' or 'I am patient, relaxed and at ease' twenty one times a day for at least twenty one days.

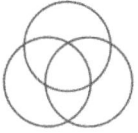

The Internal Alarm Clock

Have you been having trouble remembering to meditate? This is an imaginative tool you can construct mentally for yourself if you want to commit yourself to meditating regularly.

Imagine a clock somewhere within you that you set for a certain time of the day that suits you to sit quietly, regularly. Perhaps putting the clock in your mind would work well.

With your intention clear for this to happen, this alarm clock will go off and 'ring' within you at the time you set, and it will continue to ring until you do sit down to meditate for 5 -15 minutes. The 'ringing' feels more like agitation, a lack of ease. Your unconscious mind will obey your conscious command and do this for you.

You will slowly become agitated if you haven't meditated at the time you set or soon after. Your mind will know you haven't kept a commitment to yourself and it will nag away at you.

The only way to turn this inner alarm clock off is by sitting down to meditate.

If this agitation builds up within you, don't fear it as if something is wrong, but laugh at yourself, at your humanness, and do this thing you need to do.

Take your wonderful gift of quiet time, and love the peace you will find. Meditation is a very special gift.

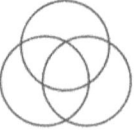

The Internal Alarm Clock Conversation

In spiritual development, we are always at the beginning. In each moment we start anew to live as well as we can. There are always new things to learn.

In every hour of the day you become a different person. You are not the same person you were half an hour ago, or will be in half an hour's time. Our vibrations, our ideas, our standards of living are constantly changing. So you must forgive yourself, and people of the past, as they are not the same people. Forgive yourself, and let them go.

That person is no longer you. How can you punish a person who no longer exists? What happened to that person is gone – release it.

When you realize this to its fullest extent, that's when you can let go of guilts, fears and resentments. Since thoughts are real forces, that has to be true or we damage ourselves.

Things in the universe definitely are unlimited, infinite. There is plenty for all. No one said you had to be poor, no one said you had to be miserable.

You are made in the image of God and there is no want in this spiritual sphere of life. There are no classes of people in the spiritual sphere, no poor, and no rich. Everyone shares the beauty that surrounds them, the beauty that was put there for all.

It can be the same for all sorts of wealth on the physical plane. Poverty has been created by man. Man has brought about sickness, unhappiness, sadness and the negative situations that surround our earth. Most important, if he has brought all this upon himself, he can also free himself of it.

The abundance of the universe has never changed. It is only man's ability to ask for it and work to create it that has changed.

If we believe in, imagine, visualize, think about, or speak about lack and limitation, we bring that in. If we believe in, imagine, visualize, think about or speak about abundance, we bring that into our lives. Thoughts are real energy and they create according to the vibrations of their energy content. I had cancer in 1983. Visualizations of destruction of the mass, of the mass being carried away, of good little cells destroying the bad ones in my bloodstream, of abundantly healthy, vibrant new cells growing in my brilliant body, I believe greatly helped the natural healing. No, I do not generalize this as the best plan for everyone's healings or cancer healings, just informing folk what worked for me and was the correct avenue for me.

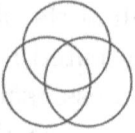

The Ball of Clarity

In times of doubt, decision making, facing those forks in life's road, this tool may help you find clear options or a solution. Use it as well as, or added to, your usual practices.

Relax, and imagine or see a ball of brilliant White Light.

As you peacefully gaze into this ball of Light ask your questions or examine your possibilities at this time. You will find things become clear for you, questions you have will be answered.

What works for some people is to have paper and pen ready to jot down thoughts, to make 'For' and 'Against' lists, for example, when needing to make a decision. Then close your eyes again, see or think or imagine the ball of White Light again, asking any further questions you may be pondering. Taking time to breathe five to ten times slowly gives the mind time to process the thoughts at every level. Keep going with this process till you are clear on your decision.

Contemplation, sitting focused on a thought or question, assists if you are still not complete.

You will indeed have clarity of thought and clarity of vision by the end of this process.

At all times when you feel your thinking is not as clear as

you would like, take out the gift of The Ball of Clarity.

Look into it and find the answers you so earnestly seek. Whatever the situation may be, you will find your answer in the Light.

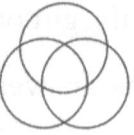

The Ball of Clarity Conversation

It seems to me that beautiful things are gifts from God, and I really appreciate and value them; sunlight through lime green new leaves, the feel of a cat's fur and his purring as he greets me with adoring eyes, a child's laughter and hugs, lovely objects brought home from travels.

We all have personal, integral gifts to use, and one of mine was creating beauty in our homes and practices. Yet I was worried I would waste previous training if I took up creating beautiful homes professionally. I didn't change professions, as it turns out, but the ideas here give sense to that wondering.

A gift is to be enjoyed. If it is no longer enjoyed, it has served its' purpose and is no longer a gift and you are under no obligation to continue with it. Use your gifts to create enjoyment for yourself. Once that gift has served its' purpose you can move on to using another gift.

If it is a gift of clothing and it goes out of fashion or it wears out, that gift is no longer applicable. If someone gives you a gift of a household appliance, sooner or later that will wear out and has to be replaced by something else.

So it is with our talents, we can move on without guilt.

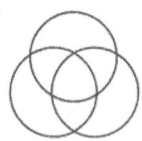

PART 2: Life Tools

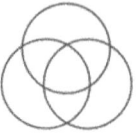

The Chrysanthemum

Please take this gift of a single beautiful, large, white and circular Chrysanthemum flower.

Study it. Look into the many petals to see how they form, how they grow, the intricacies of the petals.

See this flower as you, with each petal representing an achievement you have completed. See all the things you can pat yourself on the back for. See the hundreds of petals and think of the hundreds of instances you can be proud of, the many reasons to feel good enough.

See the end result, this amazing flower, see its beauty and look at who you are – also the end result of much work and growth. Work to make this, in full bloom, a bouquet of flowers, not the single flower you now represent.

Every time you think you are not good enough or have not done the right thing, think again. With the single chrysanthemum you have now, you have the ability to make a giant bouquet.

Feel peace and love come over you as the petals of white chrysanthemums fall gently and enfold you.

Feel the warmth of pure love. Feel the warmth of the Light throughout the days and nights ahead.

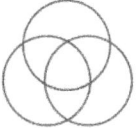

The Chrysanthemum Conversation

Each of the small things you do successfully, see them as petals on a flower and each of these eventually will make the whole, the beautiful, complete flower. See each success like this – acknowledge each flower as the bounteous success it is.

If it had just one big petal, it would indeed be ugly. You need tiny pats on the back along the way for your small successes to make the complete picture, the complete and whole success, and the perfection of the flower at the end.

Do you think the flower worries that one petal is not as long as another, or that that fact maybe gives it an imperfection? Or maybe that doesn't make it as successful or clever or bright as its fellow flowers because its petals are not symmetrical or the right shape or right design? It doesn't matter to the flower, because it knows that when it comes together in the whole, that it will be just as beautiful and successful as its fellow flowers in the bed.

Take the lesson from the humble flower. Take the lesson and allow yourself to blossom and grow in the same way as the humble flower blossoms and grows and becomes a thing of great beauty.

If the flower only aimed for one perfect petal it would be an unsightly thing, but it settles for small little victories, small little glories. The whole becomes perfection, but each little victory is perfection in itself.

It is a growing, living thing that makes a beauteous end result, as will you.

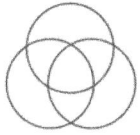

A 'Clean Slate'

I give you a clean slate or blackboard and a slate pencil or some chalk to imagine. I do this because sometime in our human existence, most of us make a life 'mess' we want to move ahead from. First we may need to erase the feelings of guilt, sadness and such. I suggest you write the 'mess' on the board and then wipe the board clean! Let it go.

I give you this tool also for you to write your positive affirmations on for you, for your future, for where you want to be in twelve months from now, twelve days from now, twelve hours from now.

Each day when you take out your slate, it will be a clean slate. There are no regrets. You can write your aspirations for the future again.

You can use this tool after the White Light exercise, and any time we need to step forward out of the past and create a new future purposefully. Daily use of the exercise really works to let us zoom ahead.

Because it is a slate pencil or chalk you can erase and change these if you choose. Your thinking is not something that is indelible. You can change your mind. You can make different decisions. It all depends on you.

Imagine using a computer with its delete button for this task if you wish. The old concept of a clean slate still applies.

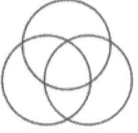

A 'Clean Slate' Conversation

How much are we held back by not feeling ourselves worthy of the good things in life? There is a huge part of our mind, the unconscious or subconscious mind, which goes about its business automatically, depending on what we have programmed it to do, like a computer.

The subconscious mind can hold old beliefs that we have taken from other peoples' words or actions, or from situations we don't think we handled well. We so often compare ourselves to others and feel we come up short. You don't do this? Let's see – are you completely happy with the physical and the spiritual person you see in the mirror? Do you judge yourself?

Do not look at what seem to be mistakes or disappointments in life, but merely see them as stepping stones to the broader picture. Learn to congratulate yourself for a job well done.

Too often people look back over the day and look at what they haven't accomplished. They will punish themselves or feel inadequate. What they should be doing is looking back at what they have accomplished and done, for these things are lessons as well. Instead of feeling badly, they should give themselves some praise to lift their self esteem, and go to bed with a healthy attitude.

There is a vast difference between having self esteem and having ego.

Ego is when some people are conceited, boastful and inconsiderate of other people's feelings. To know one's own worth and to work with that worth with humility is not being egotistical. It is understanding that the help given to them is from their intuition, so they do not become overfull of boasting and conceit.

A person with self esteem works to become all they are capable of. They do this with gratitude and humility and an appreciation of the opportunity to do their work. An egotistical person charges ahead in a boastful way and doesn't really worry about who they stand on or hurt. They crow about how great they are. That is conceit. Someone who has self esteem has no need to stand on the steeple and crow for all to see. Just by their behaviour they are truly a well balanced person; humble, grateful and appreciative of the gifts they have.

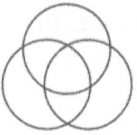

The White Rope

Imagine you are standing at one end of a white rope which extends out to the end of your life. There are lots of knots along the rope.

You can pick the rope up and work your way to each knot. As you go past each knot, you have successfully completed another lesson that you needed to learn.

This is like a guiding rope to help you make it through the rest of your life.

See it when you start to lag behind in your life, and feel yourself pulling on it, pulling yourself up, using your weight to pull yourself closer to the next lesson you must learn.

Use it as a motivator to keep moving forward.

Part 2 : Life Tools

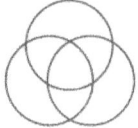

The White Rope Conversation

It used to be easy to get myself into a muddle with so much to do that I would beat myself up when I couldn't do everything in the day, to the point where not much at all was done except worry. Mental paralysis set in.

A solution in a nutshell: Work out exactly what you want to do. Work out where you want to be in twelve months. Pick the most important goal, the one that will make the most difference in your life to get to that twelve months place. Break that goal down into small actions, and get them diarized and done! Before long you can move to the second goal and it all won't be so overwhelming. A huge bunch of things to do can look like that elephant you have to 'eat', and you are going to choke on every bite.

There is no point dwelling on what you haven't achieved. What you think about comes about. If you haven't achieved, is it because you have dwelt on not achieving?

If you have been dwelling on negatives, imagine up and outside of your right eye there is a red circle with a diagonal red line through it. This is your Cancel Sign to be used whenever you catch yourself thinking a negative thought, like judging yourself. Cancel the thought by drawing a red line through the circle and think of a new, useful replacement, like how brilliant you are at <something> or that tomorrow will be perfect for that task.

Mistakes? You will make them; it is part of learning. But are there really mistakes? No, they only seem to be mistakes in the material world. In the spiritual world there are no mistakes, only learnings.

Realize that when you trip up in life, you merely skin your knees and you don't have to stay on those knees, you can rise again. Don't stay wobbling on those knees, but get up and move forward, keeping the love in your heart.

Work gently on yourself to bring yourself to full potential, to bring out all you are capable of. Most of all, love yourself so you can free yourself to love others, and be gentle with them.

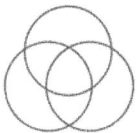

The Tall Grass

See yourself as tall grass growing strongly.

Don't fall into the habit of continually putting yourself down, mentally or verbally.

See that every time you judge yourself harshly it would be like somebody standing on that grass and bending it down to the ground.

See then the struggle that the grass must have to stand straight up once more. See that this is what you are doing to yourself when you sit in judgment upon yourself and come down hard upon yourself.

See yourself crushing that delicate grass into the ground and see the struggle that you must then make to bring yourself back up again to where you should be, standing tall.

Strive to achieve balance in your life and to improve yourself in all areas. These things are what you must keep doing, yes, but being gentle on yourself while you do it.

Whisper encouragement to yourself.

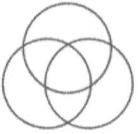

The Tall Grass Conversation

Never, ever speak in a derogatory manner about a person or their life choices. Never undermine anyone in this way. Only speak supportively in a kind way. Instead, continually send White Light for the highest good of that person.

If someone is badmouthing you, other people will see the negatives are only one way, not from you. Perhaps that person will realize people can coexist and cooperate, even if we are all very different people in our own wonderful ways.

It is usual for people to see in others what they are doing wrong, and to judge or criticize, and they don't realize it relates solely to them.

They don't realize that what they see in others, what irritates them about others, is often what they don't like about themselves, or what they don't recognise in themselves. What others are 'doing wrong' is often what *they* are doing wrong.

Listen to what you are saying and listen to your mind as well. Stop yourself, make a *Cancel* sign, which is an imaginary circle with a red line through it. Change the thoughts to *I own that*, or *that is what I am doing*, with acceptance of your OKness, anyhow.

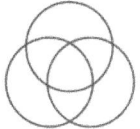

The Torch

This gift is a flaming torch, like the Olympians have. You know how they blaze. If you looked into that fire you would see the very whiteness in the centre.

I want you to take this imaginary torch and practice looking into the centre of this flame, seeing the whiteness within the centre. Use this to try to strengthen your vision of the White Light.

Use this torch to hold high every time you succeed in a victory over something you are trying to accomplish. Hold it high and take it as a victorious gesture, and then, hold it in front of you once more and look deeply within it. Practice looking at the White Light at the centre.

This you can also use to meditate upon, to see the white glow, to allow yourself to be absorbed into it and then see the wondrous things that will unfold to you.

Use this torch. Imagine holding it up as a true Olympian would. Use it for victory, and use it to increase your vision.

Go with love and peace in your heart, and be encouraged.

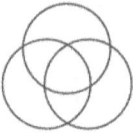

The Torch Conversation

On manifesting, it is as simple as asking and believing - as long as we commit to and work towards the goal. For anyone, for anything – as long as it doesn't cause harm of course.

Asking and believing *and not expecting the things you ask for to arrive necessarily in the form you expect them to.* That is, not putting limitations upon the manifestation, but rather, allowing it to happen as best it can, in ways it is best to do so.

Some people say *well, it hasn't happened yet, so it isn't going to happen.* They cast doubts and so they take their belief away. They have put the message out about what they want, but then they retrieve the message with doubts and that stops the manifestation from happening.

Ask and believe then *act as if* you already have what you are asking for. Create the illusion then the illusion becomes your reality. It's no use saying *I have it* then acting like a pauper, as again, you would put doubts on it. You must act as if you do have it already.

Check your belief system if you are not manifesting or have lost abundance. Do you believe you are worthy? Do you deserve it? There are many reasons why people cannot accept what is given or offered.

And of course we have to take the action steps necessary –

sitting on the couch isn't going to achieve much.

A key is: once you have abundance, it must move around to benefit others and be used. It cannot be hoarded with avarice.

This is part of your overall life plan – to set goals and do everything in your power to achieve those goals, harming no one, working for the highest good of all. Set realistic goals. Achieve these. Then you can increase the goals as you go along. It is in your planning, what you want and what you work towards that counts. You must rise and fall. You must succeed and fail according to your lessons needed and the amount of effort you put in. You are never limited by some overall plan that says, for example, you can only earn x dollars in this month and y dollars in that month.

You are assisted by people who need your help as life is for loving service. You must do the work and help them, and then find more people to serve, to grow a business. Not all will be plain sailing.

You might get a rebuff, but you think *that's my choice* and you find someone else to replace them.

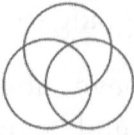

The Abundance Bowl

Imagine a lovely bowl in front of you.

This bowl you may fill with the abundance that you need or want, in whatever area you may need.

See this bowl as being your own personal possession into which you can put the abundance of material, physical and spiritual gifts that you would like to have in your life.

Imagine putting them in this bowl and carrying your bowl with you, within your heart, knowing that those things are there, and that they are there for you, and that they are achievable by you.

The thoughts would not have been implanted in your head and you would not have been able to flush them out and put them in the bowl if this were not so.

See all these things and understand that as long as you carry them in your heart, and so long as you have faith, and belief in them, and take action, then you will eventually make them a reality in your life.

Part 2 : Life Tools

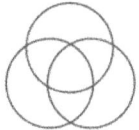

The Abundance Bowl Conversation

The thought of lack is the opposite of abundance. The actual fear of 'not enough' money, love, security, time, beauty, health, pleasure, laughter, company, wisdom, or any other of life's abundances, usually creates the reality of lack of these wonderful expressions of life's energy. Wealth and abundance are interchangeable words – wealth is far more than money – we can be wealthy in so many ways.

Mentally people don't always allow themselves to access the good things that are available because we don't feel worthy of them. We feel ashamed of things we've done or of our lives, or we think we are not educated enough or clever enough, or the effort to achieve them is too great or we simply don't know how to go about accessing the wealth. All the restrictions can be overcome given time, patience and discipline – the last two, oh, so testing of us in our humanness.

It is the having a goal to bring in the abundance that is firstly essential. Clarity about what you want is the first step. Write you outcome down. Read the goal at least three times daily feeling positive and excited, and the anticipation will move you onward. Seeing the goal complete is vital.

See it in as much detail as you can fill in; the colours, smells, the people involved. Your imagination is your guide and key to what is available to you. There are no limits, except what you will allow yourself to create with any beliefs of lack.

Break the actions needed to achieve the goal into their smallest details, eg. the phone calls on Monday, then do those. Call your loved ones. Take that course. Learn those skills. Bite the bullet. Get up early. Whatever is needed, keep your life vision clear, and your life will move to more abundance.

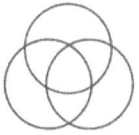

The Whistle

Every time you need to find an answer to something, take a moment and blow an imaginary whistle, then give yourself a few minutes to allow the answer to come to you.

When you want to find the right words to say, before you say the wrong ones, stop yourself short, blow your whistle then wait for the words to come to you. You will find the answers you seek. They will come more easily and readily as a result of your whistle.

The words that flow from your mouth will be more diplomatic, and may even be like the oil that flows upon the troubled waters and smooth things out.

So, keep the whistle with you. Hang it around your neck and use it as an umpire would use it.

Also use it when the desire is there for information. The whistle will stimulate your brains' grey matter to supply you with the answers you need.

This will make you laugh a little and it will also make you stop and think.

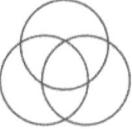

The Whistle Conversation

Go with your feelings, go with your instinct. Have faith in yourself. Watch if a bit of lack of self worth comes in to play to stop you believing in yourself. It is often there at your back, sticking its little head out and interrupting your thoughts and feelings, making you second-guess yourself and not trust yourself. Try to ignore it.

Believe you are good enough. You always have been good enough. You always will be good enough. Believe that you do not fall short of the Creators' ideals for you, only of your own ideals, and that is because you sometimes set impossible standards.

You must learn to be satisfied with yourself, with the progress you make, instead of putting impossible demands on yourself and then punishing yourself when you feel you fall short. Work more diligently on the *I am good enough*. Work with praise. As you would praise others, praise yourself. Give yourself encouragement. Do not punish yourself. Understand you are indeed human with human failings to learn from, although people feel this is a setback of some sort to be human. It is the best on offer at this time. You are here to learn how to cope, how to manage and how to survive. If you get through life doing all of that, then you have fulfilled all you are here for. This is not to be perfect, but to handle life in the best way you can with your own abilities, your own skills, with the other people around you who have both their failings and their virtues.

It is a growing time, a learning time, and a moving forward, not in perfection while you are still encumbered by human form. Perfection will come when you are no longer encumbered, when you are free.

So, now you are free to not punish yourself for not attaining perfection yet.

Do not be so serious that when you make a mistake it is a major drama for you. See it only as an inkblot that can be erased or written over. Learn to feel freer, learn to laugh more, learn to turn your problems over and ask for assistance. Once you have turned them over, then let them stay there.

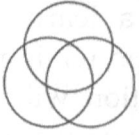

The Worry Beads

Imagine a string of brilliant and white beads in your hand.

As you touch each one and move it along, think of a positive reason to move forward in your life, and then another, and another, working along the beads.

Each bead represents one of the reasons why you want to move onwards, why you want the goals you have set for yourself, so they are your incentives for doing what is necessary, and yes, fears do leave. Then you become joyful and delighted about it all, as you know the outcomes you are working towards will be here. Use the beads often and wisely.

The beads also work well by thinking of each of the successes and positive things you have achieved in your life up to now. This reinforces you in times when courage is needed.

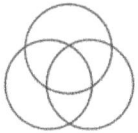

The Worry Beads Conversation

The Worry Beads tool is very helpful when laziness, fear or procrastination hits. Continue with the Worry Beads tool till you are in motion again, inspired to go forward.

This tool is also handy with eyes open as a focus tool when reading goals, and as a visual reminder of the life you are creating.

Procrastination is like the child who pushed the pumpkin to the side of the plate, and when they came to eat it, it was cold and unpalatable. It still had to be eaten.

Do not fall into negativity about your slow progress. Just start again. Spiritual development is always slow as there are no short cuts.

Each step forward is a great step indeed. See the steps as giant footprints. Rejoice in every positive event, no matter how minute it may seem to you as it is a step on the ladder.

The Source allowed humans to call themselves 'failures'.

Know you did not manifest a failure and you did not create a failure – it is only in your imagination that you have created this.

Do think of failure as a temporary lapse and know that everyone has them. Think of yourself as a winner instead and visualize and affirm this often, yes, often! Remember a time when you did succeed and focus on the success of this and what you did that worked instead of the 'failure'.

To take a more proactive role in our lives by doing what is ours to do now, no matter if we feel badly about ourselves, lifts our energy and enthusiasm and moves us out of feeling a 'failure'. Just take that first step for now. Well done!

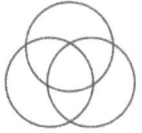

A Gift of Joy

What would make me joyful? One thing is playing with heaps of puppies.

Imagine what would make you happy and use the exercise thinking of that.

In your mind's eye, see for example a litter of chubby, playful puppies, white ones, brown ones, the odd black one playing, trundling over you, This is a fun gift for you.

Every time you are not feeling so joyful, when you are feeling down, when you are making yourself feel guilty or sad, shut your eyes and see yourself laughing and playing with these warm puppies. You will feel laughter and pleasure when you imagine this picture.

Please don't put too much pressure on yourself to the extent you stop doing the things you need to do because you are overwhelmed. You are never alone. You are never judged. You judge yourself way more than you need to. Accept yourself for the wonderfully human, perfectly made person that you are. Let your spirit lighten up and just play and be joyful.

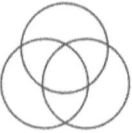

A Gift of Joy Conversation

Teach your children it is OK to express anger from time to time or they will feel guilty about doing so. Anger is an essential part of our being, but it is prolonged anger that is harmful.

It is OK to feel hurt and amazed at children's behaviour, but then do not harp on it or try to control it with anger. The child will feel confusion.

If a child feels a parent's guilt about anger then they will feel it is bad and they will have guilt feelings. The children will not live in a test tube later outside the home. They will see anger. If they hadn't learnt about anger they would think the world was evil and there was something wrong with them, that they invoke this anger in others where they hadn't at home.

Do not put impossible demands on yourself. Everyone is cross with their children at times. It is wise to be cross with your children's behavior, for if you are not cross they would not know you loved them. They would think you don't care what happens to them. Your vexation with your children is only out of concern for them.

Accept that this anger is part of the human being. Release it, let it go and move forward with greater understanding. This is perfectly all right.

You can't go punishing yourself for things in the past. That is not the way of growth; that is the way of decay. Let the past stay where it is. Look with eagerness to the future; that is the way of growth.

Understand that this is all about choices. No one is an island unto themselves. Everything a person does affects everything around them. That is all part of their choices as well, whether that is anger or happiness.

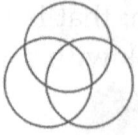

The Chariot

Imagine a speedy chariot and see yourself as the charioteer in the chariot. See your prancing steeds in front of you, leading the way, leading you on to the successes you desire in your life – personal, spiritual, physical.

See yourself charging forward, being the master of this chariot, hair flying backwards in the breeze you created, believing in yourself, and see that in this way you are the master of your own health, your own successes.

Every time you feel you are falling a bit by the wayside, see yourself as the charioteer charging on.

Don't take on more work than you enjoy and do only what you enjoy

Have fun with this. Have fun racing on to your new adventures.

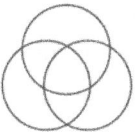

The Chariot Conversation

Don't take on more to do because you feel it is expected of you. Take on what will support your growth and happiness – and you can even choose to have fun rather that do 'the right thing'. Do only what you can do with enjoyment.

Don't respond to other people's pressure on you need to do or what is expected of you, rather see what you need to do for your own happiness and according to your own values. If it is a chore, then don't do it. If it is something you have to force yourself to do, don't do it.

Let these thoughts help you decide what to do in the future.

The mind is in every cell of the body and the emotions are the key to the mind. For example, a thought without emotion would be rather 'mindless', like a machine. The emotions make the person a person; they bring in the human element.

Affirmations are verbal or mental repetitions of what we want in life and who we are working to become. Emotions are critical for their success, for example excitement, joy and anticipation energize affirmations and take these wishes to the cellular level of your body, and to the mind. The mind takes action exactly as we ask and our cells respond.

While affirming with emotion create a picture so the mind has more to draw on. The picture gives the affirmation meaning and power. Draw a picture in the mind of what it is you are going to affirm and the mind will use it. It is not necessary to continually visualize it – once the picture is stored in the mind, the mind accesses it. This is like programming a computer; once the program is there, it is there.

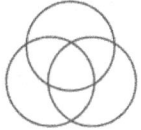

The Gold Medal

You are awarded a shining gold medal for what you have accomplished so far, and a pat on the back for the work done on yourself.

Yes, there are always challenges, but see the obstacles in front of you as just that, challenges. See them as something you can look forward to working and growing with, and learning from. See them as opportunities for growth, for new insights and awareness.

Acknowledge each job well done, however small. Do you neglect to grow your self esteem with this simple action? Celebrate your successes!

Keep on keeping on. More medals are coming!

Know that you are indeed worthy. You were born worthy, equal to everyone else in God's eyes. Let this be so in your eyes as well.

Visualize accepting an award that says you are worthy of all the good things in life.

See yourself being acclaimed as a champion for achieving good things in the physical, mental, emotional and spiritual realms and receiving a gold medal for your perseverance and commitment. See yourself as a winner. Lift your arms high in celebration and say a loud 'Yes'. Pat yourself on the back often – catch yourself doing well. In fact, give yourself gold medals enough to weigh you down.

See yourself as deserving of the gold medals, and receiving acclaim for them. Think of achievements that you have done, no matter how small. Feel the satisfaction of achievement and let this feeling lead you forward, knowing your worth.

Part 2 : Life Tools

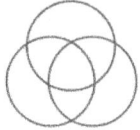

The Gold Medal Conversation

Look forward to a new venture with anticipation and excitement, not dread or fear. See it as a new challenge – without a challenge you would stagnate. Life is a series of exciting new eras to open up. Look on them gladly with anticipation, not fear. A new venture is an adventure!

Affirm you have the strength and health to do the work. Get your muscles tuned for the marathon ahead, as you would have your car tuned for the drive ahead.

Impatience impedes progress. Think: I had better slow this down so things can happen faster!

About success, the most important thing to get across to people is that you must *believe* it will happen.

Because something isn't working right now doesn't mean it won't. It just means that you have to look at things to see if there are ways of redoing what we are doing at the moment. Sometimes it just means a bit of restructuring and refocusing, but never lose the faith. That's the most important thing to get across to someone that you are speaking to about success.

Understand that you may have to go through a flat stage before you have elevation. Even a plane must run along a runway for a while before it gets up enough momentum to soar up high. Then it must level out before it can go higher. It doesn't go straight up to thousands of meters, it goes up in plateaus. When everything is adjusted, then it goes up to another height, and it is exactly the same with people. You will go to a certain level, then plateau out for a while and adjust to those circumstances before starting to build up momentum and speed for the next climb.

Imagine if the pilot gave up half way through, what would the passengers do? Do you want to be part of the ground crew that never leaves the ground? Or, will you be the pilot and take that next step and understand the necessary levels to go through to success?

Part 2 : Life Tools

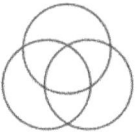

What a Bunch of Flowers!

See a huge, abundant bunch of flowers. See them in your minds' eye. All your favourites are there in profusion. Smell the smells. The perfume is just beautiful and the colours wonderful.

Take a deep breath in and allow the perfumes of the flowers to go through your nose and explode in your brain.

From that point onwards be ready for you to find that ideas begin to explode in your brain as well.

This bouquet of flowers is a gift so you can realize that you really are brilliant and ideas are just 'waiting for you' to do this exercise so they can come to you. You have everything you need within you for you to move forward in your life. Just have faith and trust.

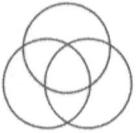

What a Bunch of Flowers! Conversation

Sometimes we can identify a mind block or belief that is holding us back, or causing us grief one way or another. Three of mine were 'too busy and too hard and I'm alone' and they have sabotaged my life often, in various ways.

I have used lots of methods to move on from these beliefs. Using the White Light a lot worked. Morning and night is the minimum I've found effective, but the more you remember to wash yourself in the clear energy of the Light, the better results you will have – peace of mind as well!

Lifting the habitual negative beliefs and thoughts out of your brain, then seeing them being put in a white bubble and floating off is a very useful tool.

Another one is to write down on a piece of paper the block that is holding you back, the too busy and so forth, and affirm that you are releasing and letting the block go. Then burn the paper, or watch its tiny pieces wash out to sea away from your life.

You could say ' I have deleted this block from my life, there are no remnants of it, it has totally disappeared'. You may have to do this a few times as these thoughts can have deep roots in our subconscious mind, that unconscious part of our mind that stores our belief systems. You have to make the subconscious mind see you are rid of the block.

Another one you could be doing is a visualization where you see yourself holding a sledgehammer with a wall in front of you. On the wall is written the grief-giving belief, like I'm alone, and see yourself bashing through those words. You have to make the subconscious mind realize that the block is eliminated and there is no reason for it to be there. Take all the wall, all the bricks away with a huge and thorough front-end loader, and dispose of them so the wall can't reform. I find the Grand Canyon a great repository. Yes, and this can be fun; if you can see the ridiculous side of these beliefs, that literally lightens the load.

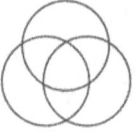

The Ball of Arcs

See a sphere, a round ball and imagine this ball rotating in the palm of your hand.

See it as if it was made up of lines, arcs and circles, rather than being solid.

Recognize that each circle, arc or line represents a quality that you wish to have within yourself, whether it is patience, compassion, understanding, or whatever it is. See that ball spinning in the palm of your hand, and understand that as it spins, it throws off these qualities and they penetrate your being.

As the ball spins, these qualities are thrown from the circle and are absorbed into you. Eventually you will look into your hand and find nothing but a blank space and you will understand that then all these qualities are there within you.

You only mentally have to spin this ball again to bring them to the surface.

These qualities are there and they have always been there, as are so many others. It just needs some little key to trigger the memory to bring them forward. Think of your ball of arcs whenever you need a particular quality and it shall be brought forward into your mind and heart once more.

Part 2 : Life Tools

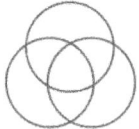

The Ball of Arcs Conversation

The people who flow through life with ease and grace have learnt from their lessons. They are walking down the track looking for their next lesson to handle, knowing it will be very different from the last one. If there is no flow in life, it is because either we haven't recognized the lesson when it was in front of us, or we are wallowing in it. The lessons unlearnt become harder over time.

Ask, have I had this lesson before? Allow your subconscious mind to bring to the fore whether you have experienced the situation before. Ask what was the lesson? Did I not learn the lesson? Why am I repeating it? Watch for a pattern in your behaviours. The simple awareness of a pattern allows us to heal and move on from it. We can choose to repeat what we're doing and not learn, or learn and not repeat. Whatever the answers, just get over it and move on! *I release, let go and move on* written or said often with acceptance, grace and a big sense of completion is a sure way forward.

Make it simple. Simplicity works. We are usually the ones hurt by holding onto past hurts. Flowing forward, looking for the next and different lesson works, and is peaceful and powerful. In there is the healing choice.

No meeting is inconsequential. Everyone you meet has some part to play, even if it may only be a minute in your life in a casual meeting in the supermarket where you stop and say hello. That is not an accident – you were meant to speak to that person. Maybe just meeting that person has lifted their spirits, has lifted them from the doldrums and made them feel better. Even though you may never see them again or ever have any contact with them again, the conversation was meant to be and has had an effect on that persons' life. Everything is for a reason.

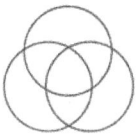

The Crown

Imagine a crown such as kings and queens would wear. Imagine this happily on your head.

See yourself as someone unique and special, someone who has been given a deal of responsibility in life but is handling that responsibility with dignity and pride; someone who now deserves to have some of the benefits that are given as a result.

At times when you feel a little less regal or perhaps a little less well, perhaps tired, perhaps overloaded, remember the crown and know that it was not given to you lightly; it was given to you to use. Take it out and put it on your head once more and reassure yourself that indeed you are special in your own ways, and that you are indeed working with the lessons that you have chosen to work with in this life.

Know that you do need to have a pat on the back occasionally from yourself. Other people can pat you on the back and that is very nice, but the most important pat upon your back is the one you give yourself. That is why you have been given the crown; so you can put it on your head and feel good about yourself to increase your self esteem and confidence.

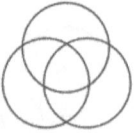

The Crown Conversation

Do you have doubt that you can do it all?

Eliminate doubt by facing it, and facing the fear that causes it. You'll always have that doubt until you face the fear.

Admit to yourself that there is nothing really to fear because there is nothing you can't handle. Say to yourself that you have complete and utter faith in yourself.

So then there is nothing to doubt. Free your mind of doubt and fear by going and doing the actions required. Hit them front on!

Go forward with trust and faith in yourself and realize you are good enough to do this, and then do it.

Be more trusting of yourself and have faith in yourself, and know that all that happens to you is for your better good. No matter how it appears at the time, it is always there for your growth and development, for your spiritual and physical life.

The decisions you make are the right ones in that moment.

Where does courage stop and foolhardy start with a decision or goal?

When you lose faith it becomes foolhardy. When you have faith it becomes courage. When you have faith in your vision it remains courage. When vision goes, it becomes foolhardy. Foolhardy includes the person who has a disease but doesn't take practical steps to handle it, however they might choose to do that. Denial postpones the inevitable – we have to face the situation, and sooner works better than later. (This is a 'pot calling the kettle black' situation – I have certainly done both of these, foolhardy and denial)

So, you must keep your vision of your future in your sights and your mind, and have the faith that this will eventuate, for it to remain on track.

There is a very thin line you have to watch that you don't cross, because once you cross that line of allowing the vision and the faith to go, then it becomes foolhardy and disaster may await.

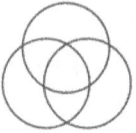

The Life Jacket

This imaginary tool is an inflatable life jacket used for water safety, in this case, for *life* safety.

It is to keep your head above water in life, to keep you up when you feel snowed under, to elevate you, to lift you, to keep you buoyant, to keep your vibrations up, to keep you happy, to keep you laughing. Is not the sight of yourself floundering around in a lifejacket enough to bring you to laughter?

Know that the decisions you make are the right ones in that moment. Work to develop more faith and trust in yourself and know that all that happens is for your better good, no matter how it appears at the time. It is always there for your growth and development, your spiritual life, your physical life.

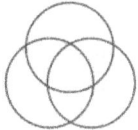

The Life Jacket Conversation

What is important to do so you can have good relationships is to delegate. Look at your priorities. See what is most important for you and learn to delegate some of the workload to others.

It is not a' cop-out'. Look around and see what is the most important thing for you to do and then delegate, for example, cooking dinner and household chores which are not all that important, compared to the raising of children or your working to your goals. Even if it takes most of your income, employ help if you need it. It is money well spent so you have *time*. Thinking only of the dollars is false economy. It is like someone who perhaps wouldn't take the right medicine for an illness they have because the medication would be too expensive, so they go with something cheaper. It is false economy because they are not getting well.

Are you in this same situation right now? It is false economy not to free yourself up to work on your goals and have more time, for example, for your relationships with your children and your partner.

Delegating to children is necessary. Children need to learn to take responsibility in life and in later years they will thank you for this. It is never too early for a child to learn responsibility.

So many people believe that desire for material possessions

gets in the way of the spiritual. God has told you it is an abundant universe and there is plenty for all, and yet, people say that as, for example Jesus was a carpenter, we all should be poor. This should not be the choice of everyone.

Another odd thought is that if you are rich, you aren't happy, yet there is so much misery among the poor, this belief can't be true. You can be just as spiritual when a millionaire as a pauper. It depends on how you use the things you are given, whether you use them for family and humanity, or for greed. Stewardship is an old yet critical value.

There is nothing wrong with amassing money for self first and to make sure families are secure. All charity should begin at home with ones' family and relatives. You can't put anyone else's house in order until yours is in order.

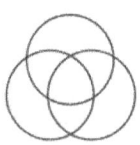

PART 3: Health Tools

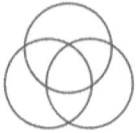

Healing Visualizations

Using the tool of the White Light, the first tool in the Energy section of this guidebook, prepare yourself, sitting quietly for healing.

Imagine flowing the Light through each organ or section of your body, allowing the Light to clear away any energy you don't want, like sadness in your heart, or anger in your gall bladder, and resentment in your liver. These may be like greyness, blackness, or feel like a heaviness, or you may simply know where to shine the Light. Any way you sense the need for healing in your body is perfect for you. You are made with your brilliant right, creative and imaginative side of your brain ready to assist you to feel calmer and less stressed, to shift any accumulated emotional baggage that gets in the way of your health and happiness.

As the Light flows through your body, allow any unwanted emotions and reactions to life situations to move down and flow out through your feet and hands and move away as a pile of black goo. Or you may wish to put it in a white or pink balloon and float it away, or give it to willing hands. Sit quietly for a few minutes as you feel calmer and more peaceful.

This clearing can be used for any sense of unease whether physical, mental, emotional or spiritual and used as often as you need or want. The key is to do the exercise until you feel a sense of greater quiet, warmth and peace as then you know the job is done, at least for now. This can take from a few minutes to, say, half and hour. I like to complete with 'and so it is'.

A fire hose surging water through the body, flushing the unwanted energies or disease out of your body can be super effective, and is fun to imagine.

A friend used her mind to see energy running freely up and down the spine of her son whose spinal cord was cut high up in his neck. She did this by imagining his spinal cord as a bunch of fibre optic cables with those bright, energetic colours flying up and down. Yes, her son did know the energy was being sent, though sadly repair wasn't possible. My point is you can use your mind through pictures, with great emotion, and who knows what can be achieved.

Use whatever will work for you to heal yourself and others. I suggest you ask for the healing to be for the highest good of all so you are not imposing your will on others.

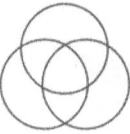

Healing Visualizations Conversation

We are only limited by our own imaginations and the limits we place on ourselves.

Albert Einstein said we use only 10% of our mind's capacity. When we are willing to open up and use some of the rest, even a tiny bit of the rest, brilliant results can happen.

And we are all capable of brilliances! This is not reliant on some IQ test in school which tells us whether we are bright or not. No. There are entirely different parts of our minds that each of us has which allow us the gift of imagination, and imagination is the key to designing our future.

See the healing happening with these tools. Trust it is happening and work towards you best outcome. I am asking you to realize that you can use parts of your mind perhaps not yet fully used – more picture making, more colours, more movement, more happy ideas for the health and the future you want. These tools are available to all of us and will make a vast difference to your life.

I believe we are powerful beyond the understanding of most of us at this time.

The first thing we need is our health so we can then create our better lives. I urge you to use the Healing

Visualizations to prevent problems and to nip small problems in the bud. I had cancer many years ago and these tools were an important part of my recovery. I used them for hours each day for months, different ones, as my fancy took me. I knew that any and all of the tools would create better energy and health in my cells in every moment. Incidentally I also had natural healers, a homeopath and a naturopath work with me. I rested and listened to healing music.

Yes, *you* can use these tools, too. *You* are powerful beyond measure.

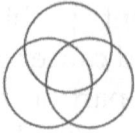

In My Palm

Imagine yourself extending your hand.

On this hand is a human form, glowing white, a small miniature of yourself, resting in the palm of your hand.

See it as pulsating in the pure White Light, in and out as you breathe. See the new, healthy, strong person you desire yourself to be. The pulsating of this figure is the Light and healthy energy moving through the miniature you.

Watch your miniature form for a while and visualize it. Feel it alive and vibrant, then take it and place it inside yourself. Let it grow and expand to full size, knowing you have implanted within yourself all the stamina, health, courage, determination and tranquility that you could possibly need.

It may take practice for you to see this, but you shall see it in time. To experience it, to feel it, will be important.

Part 3 : Health Tools

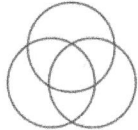

In My Palm Conversation

Being continually tired is useless .You don't enjoy your life and you don't feel bright and chirpy.

Allocate a certain amount of energy into things you are to do and give no more, no matter how energetic you feel. Only allow yourself to do so much work, then you will not create the situation where you are unable to cope with what is on your plate next day and complete those tasks.

Put the remaining energy into things you enjoy for yourself. You must allow time for what you want to do just for you. Then you will be energized to do the necessary things to combat the causes of the tiredness, for example more exercise will work. Retrain yourself and give yourself rewards to lift your energy further.

Tiredness is natural and normal when you live a busy, active life. You will become tired because it is simply time to rest; then do that, sleep.

Take a ten minute meditation which can be worth a two hour sleep. If you can slow your mind down so the body is totally relaxed in a meditation - that is very rejuvenating for you as the body will recharge itself. You are completely freeing the conscious and subconscious minds in meditation.

When you sleep, the conscious mind keeps going, rat-a-tat, rat-a- tat, going, going, going, but when you slow down in a conscious meditation, you slow it down and you will be more refreshed than when you sleep.

Start affirming that yours is a good and healthy body. Watch the words you say to your subconscious mind. Understand that when you say I am not feeling well that that is an affirmation and your mind believes it and brings it about.

Start affirming that 'my body is well, healthy and rejuvenated and

I am now being charged with positive and healthy energy', or 'I'm alive, I'm well and I feel great' or 'every breath I take fills me with vibrant health and boundless energy'. Use the breath with this affirmation to breathe in the life force. Work on your own mind.

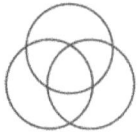

The White Flame

Imagine a large white flame within you, in the centre of your body and realize that this is the spark of health. This is the pilot light of your life energy.

Imagine its' glow, brilliant and white spreading throughout your body with you thinking, feeling, or seeing it, perhaps as white waves washing through your body. This is your life force of health.

Know your health sparkles with vitality as a result.

Daily use of this tool for a few minutes adds to our store of energy.

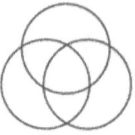

The White Flame Conversation

The key with pain relief is imagination and knowing that thoughts are real forces, real energy. Some techniques for you to use that have been useful for simple pain are:

First, simply allow the pain to drain out of the area, as if by gravity, literally into a drain that is in front of you, and wash it away.

Or it can drain out of your hands and feet, to be replaced by peaceful white healing energy.

Or see, think or imagine a brilliant White Light being focused on the area of pain. Imagine the Light zapping the pain completely away, perhaps as a laser beam, causing the pain to break up and bits of it fly off in all directions, far away from you.

Or imagine a vacuum cleaner hose extracting the pain, and then disposing of it in a white bag.

Or Pac Men, or friendly helpers of your choice, chomping the pain up. I used this with cancer to imagine the offending cells gone.

Or dig a hole with a big machine and bury the pain way down deep. Plant a favourite flower or bush on top that blooms brilliantly in your favourite colour.

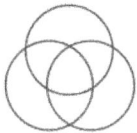

The Motivation Pills

This gift is an endless supply of imaginary motivation pills. Before you get out of bed in the morning take one of these and you will be energized and raring to go. You will be racing around to put on your sports gear so that you can start your exercise program.

The pills can be any colour that will inspire you, anything that will motivate you, take it.

This gift is also an imaginary sports whistle to blow, as if you have a referee letting you know you need to work harder at your exercise.

You know you will feel so much more alive and energetic when you do really get moving and start your day, literally on the right foot.

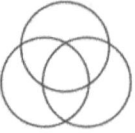

The Motivation Pills Conversation

Your health won't improve magically but with work you will achieve your health goals. You cannot concentrate on goals while your health is down. Use your energy to heal and repair, then look at other areas. Healing starts with the work on yourself – on your diet, your exercise, increasing your vibrations, your Light, your positive mental attitude, your trust, forgetting about 'mistakes' of the past and thinking of progress. You will find that these things will lead you to the next step for yourself.

Any time you need an energy top-up, imagine yourself holding out your hand and White Light flowing from the universe to you, illuminating you, filling you with an endless supply so you have it 'on tap' constantly. Know that this life energy is shared with you willingly, happily, with love.

You could give yourself at least a daily dose of healing. Used constantly it will really produce results. One thing about this, it's not the sort of thing that depletes or harms the body. The more you top it up with repetition, the more you add life energy to your body with your imagination, the more powerful it will become. It is not like an overdose of vitamins that your body can't use and can become toxic. This will stay with you forever and it will become stronger and stronger with each and every dose.

Imagine heaps of praise coming to you, which is healing.

Imagine being uplifted and having encouragement coming to you. Imagine hands underneath your elbows ready to elevate you, to lift you up, to give you a little extra energy under your wings until you learn to use them to fly quite easily yourself.

Forgetfulness is part of society now and affects young people as well. This is because you are all busy and active and you do have lots to remember. Think 'I have perfect recall, I have perfect memory'. Work with these affirmations instead of 'I can't remember'. Erase that from your mind, reprogram your mind.

When someone says 'that's what's to be expected, that's a sign of old age', erase these words. Put in the good thoughts, don't dwell on the unnecessary negatives. Let's drive forward always with positive expectation. One tool that is effective for me when I want to remember a fact is to say to myself "I am as sharp as a tack". I carry on with my life and the answer soon comes.

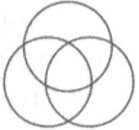

Dancing Free

Imagine yourself leaving your body, putting on your dancing shoes and dancing free, shaking off the worries and woes that overwhelm, the trials and tribulations. Experience the true meaning of freedom as you dance amongst the clouds.

See yourself floating easily and dancing. Have the stars as your dancing companions. Have the clouds as the floor beneath your feet. Feel the freedom that goes with this experience. Think of times of joy, laughter, peace and tranquility.

This visualization you can do within your mind when you feel burdened down or snowed under or less than perfect. You will lighten up.

There will be plenty of times you will be able to use your dancing shoes to lift your spirits, to energize you, to give you patience and help you maintain your strength, both physical and spiritual.

This will help you greatly in times of stress. Spend a few moments dancing freely. When you return you will be able to handle the situations more effectively without being tied up in emotions like anger or frustration, for you will have experienced freedom. You will have given the body time to calm down and the nerve ends to settle. You will see things in a different light. A lot of the frustration will have gone. If not, which is rare, do the exercise again, or choose another tool to use till you do feel calmer.

Whatever you do, don't give up on yourself and your ability to change your life for the better as I know that with a bit of patience and practice, we can all do this.

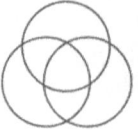

Dancing Free Conversation

It is possible to dance through life, and when you stub your toe on life it doesn't hurt as much if you are dancing. You can make it a jig or a waltz, or make life drudgery, it all depends on you.

For greater health, imagine yourself dancing joyfully in brilliant White Light, the Light filling your bones for strength, and each area or organ of the body in turn being filled with the energy of life and vitality. See rejuvenation, regeneration and revitalization happening as Source Power fills the body. Access the energy of the universe for your body's sake.

The old Chinese proverb 'an oiled gate never squeaks' applies to your joints. By exercising you are oiling your body so you won't squeak in old age. Or think of yourself like a battery. If you aren't put on a charger and recharged with exercise, you will go flat, and aren't you finished with that feeling?

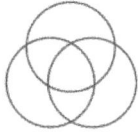

The Flotation Tank

As you get into bed, see in your mind's eye that you are lying down in a brightly lit flotation tank. This is large rectangular metal container filled with perfectly warm water that people relax in for healing of muscle soreness and tiredness, and to just feel good.

In that tank you are surrounded by brilliant white water and you are floating gently in it.

As you float freely feel the healing power of the water so you know that as you are going to bed you are getting into a healing chamber of White Light.

Know that it is healing you, that it is allowing you to move freely, that it is allowing your food to be used well and it is helping you regenerate and stay young. Use it every night. You will feel the benefit.

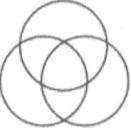

The Flotation Tank Conversation

Let contentment live within your heart and let that be your aim this day.

No task is for you to walk alone; you are never alone. You are part of the vastness of the energy of the universe, created from the same source as everyone else, and networked together. So we are all equal.

All you can ask of yourself is to be the very best you can be, but, being human and still encased in human form, you need something to aim for and if perfection is what you need to name as your goal, by all means do so. Do not blame yourself or whip yourself when you fall short of that perfection.

Understand that life, parenthood, all parts of life are learn-as- you- go. There are no directions, there are no courses, and there are no books that can truly *make* you a better parent or person. These are things you experience and learn in your day to day life as you go along. It is a learning and growing experience, and however you handle your growth, you are handling it in a way that is right for you at that time.

Nowhere is there ever a book written about the right way to bring up a particular child, for each child is different and must be handled differently. Each parent is different and has a different set of emotions and personality traits. If such a book was written, it would be useless, for it would apply to one person only and that would be the author and perhaps the authors' child.

Instead of berating yourself, pat yourself on the back and say

I'm doing the best I can, the best I know how, and that is all that can be expected of me. Surround yourself continually in the White Light, the energy of the Creator, and send light into the children and the people in your life and this will help you all through the challenges.

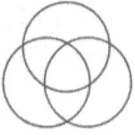

The Angels' Wings

Picture for yourself the most beautiful pair of angel's wings.

Strap them on so you can fly freely above the earth and your problems, so you can look down and see these problems from a different angle, from a different viewpoint.

These wings will also help you soar to the heights to which you wish to soar, and keep you up there. You don't want to stay down here with all the people who are looking at doom and gloom and disaster. You always want to be up there feeling elevated and removed from all the turmoil and worry that seem to be around. This is a good place to be.

Or you could fly away to a fluffy white cloud where you can sit back in comfort and relax whenever you feel you need to do so.

Your lovely angel wings will take you anywhere you would like to go. Any place that you desire is there for you to relax and enjoy. Want to travel? Imagine your wings transporting you to faraway places, giving you a relaxing holiday on a white beach lapped by azure water, or smelling the exotic fragrances of a spice bazaar, or riding a camel in a far off desert.

Allow your wings to carry you to the heights you desire, keeping your faith and trust in yourself and your Creator.

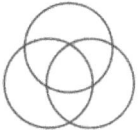

The Angels' Wings Conversation

A picture of the aura, the energy body that surrounds the physical body, is a picture of the real you. The aura holds the mental, emotional and spiritual energies you put out. It reflects every thought, every emotion, every emotional scar you are carrying.

The physical body is a mirror of these energies and your health level to an extent reflects the way you have been choosing to think and feel in each moment.

The physical body is the uniform the soul wears. Let's call it the Soul Suit. In it you live and experience this human state. If a limb is removed, for example, it is still spiritually there as we feel the phantom limb and Kirlian energy photography shows it is still there.

Kirlian photography is a collection of techniques that capture and show us the phenomenon of electrical discharges that come out of living things.

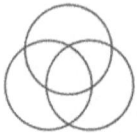

The Box of Stardust

This gift is a box of sparkly white stardust for times when you are feeling a little low or a little tired. Imagine taking the stardust out of the box and sprinkling some on yourself.

As we are appealing to the child within you, imagine how a child would react if they had been sprinkled with stardust. They would feel wonderful and magical and brand new.

Allow yourself to experience that. Allow yourself to experience things in the way a child would experience them. Allow yourself to *be* as a child. Feel the excitement and joy, the love and laughter, as a child would. Allow the stardust to sink into you and perform miracles in you.

This stardust can also be used on other people. Combine it with the White Light and see the transformations that will take place.

A very special gift for you.

Part 3 : Health Tools

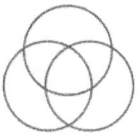

The Box of Stardust Conversation

A common situation with parents is 'at the moment I am giving so much to others and receiving very little back, and I'm exhausted'.

Think of this as sometimes being necessary, and maybe it would help if you don't look at immediate returns. Think of this time as planting seeds for a wonderful crop you can't harvest for some time.

You could look at the little things that are given back to you rather than looking for the big things. After a year of detached stand- off from our adopted 11 year old daughter, she reached out and touched my knee at her birthday breakfast. No eye contact, but a touch. That is still a high point in my life and a moment that sustained and encouraged me.

The fact that you may feel taken for granted is a compliment in itself. To know that the children feel secure enough with you to take you for granted is good. That is a giving of trust and love to you. You are so important to them that they can take you for granted. If they didn't feel that comfy with you, you really would have something to be concerned about.

Children have another way of loving. Not being able to

do it in a way that parents perhaps may expect them to, but in their own way, they are giving of themselves as they give of their love and trust and their warmth in so many ways. Look for these and be reassured.

Parenting. Oh, my. We do our best and still I made messes of this job, seemingly regularly. 'I shouldn't have been so cross, I should have given him more time to explain, I really should have been more patient, I should have cuddled them more, I should have …. etc. At the time, in the middle of the apparent hugeness of it all, my 'shoulds' of myself were rampant, made worse because I could see what I was doing, and I judged myself harshly every time. That the children (three older, adopted) didn't love me as I wanted and expected was painful, and I saw that as my failure as a Mum, till I was given the advice above. Then I started to use the tools to calm down, by using them as I wanted and felt I needed to. I learnt to step back and have quiet moments, for example, on an imaginary cloud, to detach for a little while and come back to my equilibrium, then come back to the children and life and handle the situations more quietly and purposefully. Did I manage this every time? No, but without these tools our family would have had a more rocky time by far. I can only urge you to use the tools as they will simplify and, yes, beautify your life. This is my wish for you. With Love.

About the Author

I was one of those tomboys who fell out of trees, over gates and pushed my body to its limits. After a gymnastics accident while doing my Physical Education teacher training, I was told by medical specialists that I would be in a wheelchair before I was twenty one. When my back really did fail at just twenty one years old, both legs were not moving, some organs were not functioning well.

My father suggested I visit a 'quack', the first chiropractor in the Bega area of southern NSW, Dr John Parker. I will be forever grateful to Dr John as I hobbled out, very gingerly, but on my own feet.

Over the next few years as my husband John and I travelled and worked on various continents I had acute back problems, and again and again chiropractic helped me out of my pain. In Toronto, Canada in the mid 70's, my husband and I trained as chiropractors. I learnt about keeping the spine, and the body structures as freely moving as possible to actually prevent these episodes. This was marvelous, life changing information. I returned to Australia with John and we practiced in rural NSW, then in Brisbane. We started a coaching and mentoring business called The Centre for Powerful Practices in 1991 to mentor chiropractors and other health practitioners.

In 1983 cancer showed up. I am fortunate to have believed that the body is built innately to heal itself, that the frequent reason it doesn't stay healthy or heal itself is interference or stress of some kind or kinds. Natural healing was my choice and I acknowledge the caring assistance from excellent naturopaths, healers and from great books and courses.

The years had flown by and we were thirty nine by the time my intuition kicked in to adopt our children. We found two older brothers in an orphanage in Chile, and later their sister, who were undoubtedly our children. An interesting time was had by all of us for a few years, sorting out the new family. Now, they all have families of their own and are blessing us in so many wonderful ways.

I have spoken internationally and locally on health and energy and have been given humanitarian and recognition awards. I have learnt from my experiences, studied widely, listened to many people and filed away myriads of useful tools, options and ideas that get results. I am committed to being accepting, encouraging, empathetic and extremely practical. I believe I have an understanding of and compassion for the human experience we are all living.

I have been focused on teaching and coaching within the chiropractic profession. Stress is such an enormous drain on peoples' health, energy and quality of life, and it is so widespread, that relieving and preventing stress is where I need to focus from now on.

VISIT OUR WEBSITE
www.StresstoStrength.com

Great Tools in Helping People Regain Control...

"Dr Judy Hinwood is a heart-felt person with great experience and knowledge in the field of healing. Judy has been of tremendous help to myself and my family in matters pertaining to emotional and spiritual well-being. 10/10 for great tools in helping people regain control of their health in every way."

-Dr Nicholas Armitage
Hawthorne, QLD, Australia

Working With Judy is Life Changing...

"Judy is an outstanding coach and mentor. I have found her insightful and thorough. She will not allow you to get away with using less than the magnificent potential she sees in you. Working with Judy is life changing, it will take you to levels you never thought possible."

- Dr Pauline Walsh
Mooroolbark, VIC, Australia

LOOKING FOR A SPEAKER FOR YOUR NEXT CONFERENCE, SEMINAR OR WORKSHOP?

You can contact Dr Judy Hinwood or Dr John Hinwood at info@StresstoStrength.com

for speaking engagements.

Drs John & Judy Hinwood
Stress to Strength
PO Box 4125
Forest Lake Qld 4078
Australia
Phone: + 61 7 3879 0069
Fax: +61 7 3714 9700
Email: info@StresstoStrength.com
Website: www.StresstoStrength.com

Call or email us to order additional copies of this book

www.ingramcontent.com/pod-product-compliance
Lightning Source LLC
Chambersburg PA
CBHW071707040426
42446CB00011B/1959